Perceivers Window

GATEWAYS THROUGH MY SOUL

POETIC MESSAGES

Denise McGrath

BALBOA.PRESS

A DIVISION OF HAY HOUSE

Balboa Press books may be ordered through booksellers or by contacting:

Balboa Press
A Division of Hay House
1663 Liberty Drive
Bloomington, IN 47403
www.balboapress.com
844-682-1282

Because of the dynamic nature of the Internet, any web addresses or links contained in this book may have changed since publication and may no longer be valid. The views expressed in this work are solely those of the author and do not necessarily reflect the views of the publisher, and the publisher hereby disclaims any responsibility for them.

The author of this book does not dispense medical advice or prescribe the use of any technique as a form of treatment for physical, emotional, or medical problems without the advice of a physician, either directly or indirectly. The intent of the author is only to offer information of a general nature to help you in your quest for emotional and spiritual well-being. In the event you use any of the information in this book for yourself, which is your constitutional right, the author and the publisher assume no responsibility for your actions.

I appreciate all your professional input and editing and enjoy working with Brandon Bayne and Balboa Press ☺

ISBN: 979-8-7652-4233-9 (sc)
ISBN: 979-8-7652-4234-6 (e)

Print information available on the last page.

Balboa Press rev. date: 06/05/2023

Introduction

The title of this book was divinely inspired through moments of light and dark periods in my life. I was given these poems that could be referred to in various ways but my feeling is that my connection to the Universe gifted me with what I would refer to as automatic writing evoked by my emotion and thoughts around my experiences be it past, present or what may come (Wishes Dreams)

These poetic messages were not just for me but for the many and will be perceived in various ways by each person who reads them from their own thoughts and feelings. My hope is that these poetic messages bring a positive and transformative healing to the mental and emotional self, to not feel alone to feel our emotions and know that that's healthy not weak. We all go through similar experiences that vary in degree, one example would be abandonment feeling alone not wanted. Every human has felt abandonment at some point be it a brief moment in a school yard where no one wanted to play with you to what could feel like endless lonely nights.

These poems that I write are evoked by my emotions and spill out onto the page so quickly that I write them out with bursts of thought driven by my feelings, I write until I've reconciled or realize I need to work on healing, figuring out that loving yourself through the ups and downs is crucial. I started this journey almost 6 years ago after my life as I knew it changed in a flash

My poems can be contemplative to urge us to go within think and feel to get in touch with our selves and others, to be empathetic and understanding with our selves and others, open to perspective and that we will never have all the answers and that we weren't meant to

Humbly and sweetly in service to all that is
Denise McGrath

Opening

Where to start? from the beginning is what we generally
say but I will start from where I am, the last poem I've
written and travel backwards. Hang on these poetic
messages come not in order but where they are
intended to be order out of chaos each
it's own individual message

Quiet and Peace

Do we ensure our peace and quiet when we
need it or do we allow others to deplete it

Stop obligating your time to all else it's time to give to self

From a place of peace and quiet there we can get in touch
with the highest, the higher part of our self the most high
wants to connect with you, your self one in the same

When your ready the All awaits

Optimistic

Being optimistic, be optimistic about love be
optimistic about life be optimistic about your wishes
and dreams this is what brings them in

In this mindset it changes everything, you walk in assurance
suppressing the minds chatter of negativity and doubt

No past pains standing in your way just your
dreams in the forefront for today and the next

A new start give thanks, we are blessed

The Sun and Moon a union soon to be expressed

Temperature

Cold and crisp can make you feel alive
but not for long periods of time

A warm fire burns slow the flames get higher
blue and orange the thought of snuggling up
with someone you love feels warm within

Can't take my mind off of him

Indoc

Indoctrination may not serve us in the
here and now, has it ever?

A lifetime of very specific rules and regulations if
these can't be changed discord, stagnation

How can we grow and expand if were always
adhering to the same old plan

This effect in governments, societies, personal
situations can lead to stagnation, fixed situations

Were told stick with the plan stick with the way but if
change is inevitable how does that serve us today

Governments need to change for the benefit of the people,
societies of free thinkers, people allowed individual
freedoms respecting each others opinions with feelings

The only thing that is constant is change when
we push against it things remain the same

Doing the same thing over and over again and expecting
different results just doesn't work its broke

The question is how does that serve us, the question remains

On my own

All the skills I have learned since 2018 were
not in vain but propelled by my dreams

2023 is to be decisive to say yes no time
to mull over wonder, guess

Realizations eventually hit even with a
water sign who's emotional at best

My dreams I will follow I've worn many
hats, all meant to teach me I got this

Love, creativity with the pen I express
I'm open and willing, I got this

Loving Connection

Passion isn't all of it, love goes much deeper
it's not surface it's everything

The things you can feel a connection natural
and real it's warm its joy it's strong worth
fighting for many songs not just one

The depth of love is true not easy but it's worth all emotions
the thoughts given, when you rest in it feels like heaven

Emotion

Showing emotion is one of our greatest strengths
but life our upbringing told us to suppress

It's as if we were locked in an emotional prison stand
proud be tough no giving of the emotional
stuff

The release of emotion unlocks the prison door it's as
if we finally stepped outside the sun warm deep breaths
fresh air clear, hard to feel from a locked up place

Yes balance is required the middle path, to much emotion or
none at all can leave us empty, emotional turmoil or void

Valentines Day

Valentines day was just another day, yet with the
awareness that love is present 365 days a year

I am happy and content being where I'm at on
this day because love is always present

Love of family love of my dog love and fond memories of those
who are gone love of friends, it all circles back around again

I'm not diminishing this day that may mean more to Lovers
I'm just not there on this day and within me that's ok

I look forward to a day of red hot passion but
love has to be the underlying action

I've asked cupid to shoot someone in the ass but
until the arrow strikes I'm ok where I'm at

Hope all had a good Valentines day and if you
didn't feel love I'm sending it your way

It's OK

Are we done being hard on ourselves do we
not know how very special we are

We are hardest on ourselves our own worst critic in our
head imagining what we believe we have perpetrated

Do we not realize the other agreed to dance no one person
should shoulder it all talk it out work it out then it will grow

It's not what we have but who we are, we
all shine bright a beautiful star

I see beyond the surface I see inside do you
not know it's reflected in your eyes

I stand before you as you approach and want you
to know we can work this out, you don't need
to go

It's safe for us to speak from our hearts we will
see look into each others eyes you know me

The Universe my school

I write from a place of emotional intelligence
the Universe the stars my school

I feel I create and in that space I am my own guru

My guides are my teachers I go within and take a seat in
class, the material they present to me is heart mind math

The lesson is to balance the two not always easy simple to do
yet worth the work endless study the etheric my study buddies

Lesson #1 ground yourself for on this planet
you don't want to be unbalanced

They'll eat you alive think you spread lies if
all you can talk about is your school

You were meant to be in both places
but may be viewed as a fool

Take heart be compassionate never place yourself above
another because we all reside where we choose to

All of us a divine creation, all of us birthed in this
place be loving be mindful, walk in grace

Free Will, the beauty of it all

His Walk

He's passionate he's spicy he walks assured

He walks forward to get it done stand aside don't run

The heat I feel on all levels he lights me on fire, his
steps the heat wave I feel as he walks by me

If you can't take the heat get out of the kitchen
don't stand in his way, he's sexy strong self assured
yet soft and funny an enigma, I'm intrigued

Oh My…

Old Shoes

Hanging on to an old pair of shoes but
never wearing them hmmm

What are we resisting why don't we let go, could
it be we don't know how the new shoes will
feel

They were comfortable made my feet feel good until
they started pinching with every step I took

I want to let them go they use to feel so good

I ran I jumped I danced all night the feeling the
memories were meant to fade, it's ok a new pair
of shoes will fit better

You've outgrown the other

Change in the blink of an eye

I was married for over 30 years felt like
I wasn't seen or taken seriously

I believed he only saw half of me but then again from
where I am maybe I was only half back then

I've always dreamt and fantasized to a
serious person it looked unwise

Its inevitable that we grow some fast some slower

At the core of who I am a loving mother a loving
friend a caring wife to no end, led by emotion all
my life I may not of been his perfect wife

Those we cross paths with can be a catalyst for change
good bad or indifferent expansion just the same

Don't regret your past it made you shaped you and blessed you
with all the experiences and memories that created your now

May these be the best days of the rest of our lives

Love Recognized

I want a love that stays, we feel like home

He loves me just as I am and I him

The warmth from my heart is felt he doesn't question it he
feels it deeply no question he will want to always keep me

We feel each other so deeply we are the truth,
love expressed our smiles say so much

We hear one another, conversations can get deep
but never lost our own minds we keep

We flow we know we don't question us
we laugh feel joy just being us

A look is all it takes our eyes see into each others
soul even if we don't consciously know

We reach for each other longing to come together,
so powerful the embrace holding hands the simplest
touch, our souls recognize each other as love

No words can define this no words needed
we trust for we can always feel it

I don't want much I just want it all I know
this love was never impossible

The Water

The sand beneath my feet the stick in my hand
the patterns I draw sent out to all lands

This energy created infused with love light and peace
will reach all shores in my heart this I feel

The waves carry this energy the ocean it's vessel
the intention to cover a world I believe to be
special

May every man woman and child all life on
earth feel the love this energy sends forth

Some Days

Some days, why is life so complicated contemplative irritating

Thoughts consuming wanting to be over it

How can we feel so good then all of a sudden crash
and burn a winding road to many turns

From this place we seem to create the most profound feelings
good or bad we write them down spit them out happy or sad

Tomorrow a new day, knowing yesterday has gone away
hoping today will be good but then again who knows
what it will bring, it's ok either way a new day assured

Beauty

True beauty grows over time it comes
from within then out it shines

A beautiful heart a beautiful mind the most
precious gifts developed over time

Passion

Do we seek passion release pheromones
thinking it's love then left alone

An indication the conversation pay close attention listen

Very quickly you will discern the answers you are seeking

Turn Around

Do we drive each other into the arms of
another will we ever take flight

Like the Phoenix burn it down spread
your wings turn around and see

With clarity you and me

Charming

Charming sexy full of shit is definitely not a
relationship all you can expect is passionate

If you want a loving relationship and you know
this to be true relax let it find you

Emotional Accountability

I'm not a liar I say what's true the energies
can shift all depending on what you do

No action tired of waiting not going to
sit in sadness contemplating

Decided to have fun take a chance feel good
dance, doesn't change what my heart feels but not
in a commitment regardless of how I feel

With no reciprocation or taking account how could
one feel betrayed when they don't give out

Imbalance emotional void can take a serious toll

Communication with no response may
have given you what you want

So step up and say what you want what you need if you
can't do that let go of me, I can feel your energy

Imposing Blocks

Beware of blockages that arrive wake up open your eyes

You'll know soon enough if you go within and trust

Just look at it as fun that won't last you needed time
to simply laugh, just be aware of where your at

If the fun is over the thrill is gone negative
behavior same ol song, carry on

Chances are you already knew it's ok because
you grew, be creative you've got things to do
maybe the Universe was testing you

It's ok you wanted to laugh if only for a moment

Detrimental Empathy

Detrimental empathy what does that mean?

Is our heart misplaced to make sure someone's ok
or is it ourselves were trying to heal that day

Do we take the time to feel from deep within
knowing we don't need to repeat again

Can we heal our self not relying on all else peace within self

I believe we can, from the peace we can feel our heart and
soul wanting to express what feels good and what does not

Acknowledge it all your doing the best you
can your light heart will shine again

Fearless Emotion

Love starts with being fearless and authentic saying
what you feel acting on what you want

If you can't be real if you can't realize you will change
ever expanding rolling with it then you will stagnate
overthink it, create in your mind what you think
might happen create realities that don't even exist

Boundaries what does that mean drawing a line in the sand
creating a barrier a barrier against what? Your feelings
their feelings that term has been abused and over used

Good luck communicating from an
authentic place with boundaries

Acknowledgement of Moods

The struggle to transform from the dark spaces to light

Persevere don't give up the fight

Not all can be accomplished with soft kindness
at times the light can blind us

Going into the darkness to sit in silence knowing what
you want what you need in darkness the brightness

We will always fluctuate between the two creation
can occur in both reborn again anew

Speak it into creation only you can find it

They called me Grace

I am gracefully ungraceful and it's just who I am
use to trip over my own feet again and again

Grandma use to say stand up straight point your toes
out and I'd just carry on without thought move about

I was joyful light hearted lived in every moment
found no value in being groomed, ran around
outside at night looked at the moon

The innocense I've kept within every
once in awhile it peeks out again

I am Woman

"I am woman hear me roar" I don't keep score

Such behavior I don't need I am assured in me I
give from the heart because it feels good to me

No agenda no games just who I am

In the past I felt unworthy to receive then
I started thinking about me

Funny enough we can be the last on our
list until one day we say screw this

"I am Woman hear me roar" meow

Not Accepting Less

"You get what you give" A quote that speaks volumes

Don't keep giving if you don't receive no need to
beg or plead if it doesn't happen walk away no
more time for manipulation, mind games

In a place of constant waiting being ghosted
being shunned realize it's control run

If these are the indicators do you want it? Ask that
question look deep inside take time close your eyes

My answer would be no, if I'm not treated
with love then it's time to go

Joy and loving interaction is what I will be attracting

Life's to short to sit around waiting waist
no more time contemplating

Compassion

I'm not here to pick anyone apart first and
foremost I have a loyal true heart

Overly emotional does not benefit me even though being
sensitive hasn't always served me it had created a defensiveness

Be not overly defensive compassionate yes don't forget to be
compassionate to self then naturally it happens with all else

Judgement

Let us not compare or judge

We could miss out on love

We all do it, the trick is to be aware and correct it

Stand in Loves Strength

I may be viewed as kind and sweet
understand I'm not asleep or weak

I will always treat others with kindness until they
cross a line I will not stick around a waist of time

One can not control the uncontrollable but one can share
respect care and love, welcomed energies embraced no thugs

Ego

We all have ego but to what extent are we even aware of the
trauma it can create for ourselves, from childhood to present

We act like we don't have choices yet we always do, they
require decisions that finally serve you, the highest good too

Staying in unhappiness out of obligation is a choice
we made that we believe others created

When we fight what we want that our soul longs to be
or do were not only hurting ourselves but others too

Resentment distain intolerance negativity at every
turn a miserable situation for all concerned

To stay where we are because it's what we know
is never a good reason just ask your soul

An out of balanced ego can make us feel safe yet
stuck repetitive behaviors not willing to adjust

The soul suppressed little joy and happiness mostly numb

To ever grow and expand is to feed our souls be assured
we will never want to know it all, a divine road

Dreaming by the Water

I sit by the water often and dream

I find peace in my fantasies, filled with lovely feelings

I remember the laughter we shared more often then not, let's
recreate that place relax into each other relax into our thoughts

We can let go of the rest it doesn't serve
us, blocks our happiness

Silver Curls

Thinking about the silver curls at the back of your neck

Wanted to run my hand through the curls feel
your neck, not the time or place, not consent

I can fantasize I can visualize I can imagine
it would be a pleasant surprise

Thoughts of you linger, brings a smile to my
face imagine your response as you pull me close
letting me know I'm what you want

Side by Side

I will not walk behind I will walk beside

I will not stay in the shadows but stand in the light

I will be me and you will be you and in this
togetherness there will be truth

We will face the darkness together as well as
the light and in it all we'll be more then alright,
together in a true and loving relationship

New in the year

Coming into this new year awake or asleep
or maybe somewhere in-between

What is it we want to release what is it we want to do, achieve

In my case I believe many a thought brought me to my knees,
physically sick near the end the Alchemical process my friend

Transmutation of the physical self can be
shown when we refuse it ourselves

Sick to my stomach the physical side a message to open
my eyes pay attention are you taking care of your mental
emotional and physical self or distracted outward instead
of in, how is that serving you and to what end

My solar plexus built up energies suppressed my
throat chakra words not spoken but kept

Were given assistance guided to listen our
intuition, free will never stripped away

For in the end it's in your hands to always do it your way

Our higher self the guiding light do we turn
it off when we want to be right

Regardless of how we've been there's
always a chance to start again

Happy New Year

I See You

You make me smile deep inside even when your abrupt

There is nothing you need change I want you so much

Do you understand I feel all of it even your scars

I feel your brilliance mind body and soul how exactly I don't
know, some things can't be explained just wanted you to know

It's ok to be comfortable with this, it's not a
weapon it's a loving deep connection

And yes they do exist

Who I Am

Who I am today is not who I was yesterday

No need to morn it no need to miss it growth
is always needed good or bad experience

I have resolve I know what I want only getting
stronger with each passing moment

Project not to far forward waist no time looking
back as much as you can be in the moment, at
last

Let the Lotus unfold at it's natural pace don't stop
it don't force it allow it's opening with grace

New Memories

Let's drop the past it's getting old reach
out take my hand let this unfold

The past can't be undone but making new memories can be fun

Regret can stop us from following how we
feel, the stagnancy of the karmic wheel

How can a wheel ever turning become stagnant,
it happens with the same repetitive actions

If we want change create it or sit in the same
place and merely contemplate it

Hunger

I want someone that is hungry for me
mentally emotionally and physically

I want all that

Blunt I can be yet in grace I can stand the only
one who will match me is a powerful man

Powerful in love a powerful mind an independent
soul that has grown over time

Together we can continue to grow,
meeting of the mind and soul

Self

"Know thy self" powerful words

From that place comes a peace

No need to make all others happy, that is
for them it comes from within

Fulfillment in self, no external expectation of who you must be

Just be yourself a satisfaction like nothing else

Dreams

Do you remember your dreams? I do not my
emotions become strong thoughts

Very rarely do I awake and take the time to contemplate

Throughout my day strong feelings roll in so
strong they come from deep within

I suppose it's a day dream not at night when I
sleep, all I know are these dreams I keep

I feel them deeply strongly, truly as if they are written in
the stars I look up and wonder is that where you are

Can I reach you have I touched you all
I know is I long to love you

I want it All

Intimacy without emotion a lonely road I'd
rather be lonely and so alone I chose

A year gone by not a touch a kiss nothing to long for
or miss I'd rather have it all then feeling amiss

I was fighting my demons working through past hurts
from time to time defensive acting as if I wasn't hurt

I believe I'm at a place where my past hurts have
faded ready to express myself fresh elated

One foot in front of the other my dreams still alive
I know this within and when I look in his eyes

Our own minds game

Guilt and shame is a self imposed game the minds prison

Regret an energy that leaves you feeling less

Other's that mind your business by imposing
what they believe to be right or wrong if it's
not how you feel you can leave it alone

We are not obligated by those who want to impose or control
trust you're a good person and walk your own road

Happy and Grateful

I'm not vengeful I'm not hateful I'm
generally happy and grateful

Why because it serves me and my heart

Yes I can get sad and disappointed even
when I don't choose to show it

In private I work through my sadness there I
feel comfortable wrapped in my blanket

Staying in that sadness is not where I choose to
be I want to believe in better days, happy

I have no motives my feeling aren't fake viewing positive people
this way a big mistake, one may miss out on something great

Mostly positive is where I choose to be, people
like me aren't always taken seriously

My strength of self my love of all else makes me feel good

I will be me looking at the glass half full and
wishing all well because it feels good

Deep Diving

Deep within the recesses I can feel your scars
I'm familiar I know who they are

Betrayal lies the pain we've been through I
know how they act I've been there too

I've gone in search of my inner light hoping and
wishing that again it will shine bright

Love my compass my faith at times shaken but from
everything I've gone through wisdom taken

I'll not force another in what to do for in each of us our own
light can shine through only we can make it come true

Shine like a Star

That Smile

That smile of yours if even for a split second fills me with joy

Confirms that what my heart feels is true and real even if in
brief moments I doubt you I doubt myself realizing something
so powerful brings a little fear, is this to good to be true

I find in your presence life is content even if your having
a bad day a bad week my thoughts for you sweet

You've seen my moods as well, doesn't mean it's all
going to hell just means there are moments where we
don't feel great doesn't mean that's where we stay

My journey for over a year was solitary to become
clear, clear with my self knowing I don't need
another but my heart knows your my lover

I feel it I imagine it I dream it and can't wait to be in it
with you on all levels my heart has been given to you

If healing and a gentle touch is needed we know
we can do it not blind we can feel it

Adventure of a lifetime

An adventure of a lifetime together

Been single a free spirit learned a lot even when I didn't see it

Done with the parental road my children are grown can hold
their own, loved it when I was in it now they no longer need it

I'll always be Mom just a phone call away
but now it's time for me to play

Alone on this road not so thrilled I have so much love to give

I want a partner who's a free spirit to share
this adventurous road, together in it

Adventures large or small loving life in the simple
things star gazing in our back yard conversation
every now and then see something amazing

Why stand on the shore waiting hop in
the boat make life amazing

Time after Time

In this 3rd dimensional space and time I want
to get to know you, no reason or rhyme

In the 5th dimensional space I already know
you yet we can't stay in that place

On this planet it's all new even if some how I remember
you, just a flicker a comfort not understood maybe
we were together and it was beyond good

Time after time did we come together how do I
explain the comfort how do I know what I feel
is real

We may never know the answers and in this
time of now does it even matter

I want to know you even if I do there's
something special about you

Moderation

Moderation where is it extremism what a mess

We should take advice from a Buddhist

No moderate right no moderate left leaves
the people in combative distress

When did we stop listening to each others point of view
doesn't mean we must agree just simply listen to

Do we have all the answers no we don't unless
you speak to someone claiming to be woke

If we think we have nothing to learn or gain this
is going to remain a very adversarial game

The people united not divided respecting
each other open minded

Whole for now

I am whole as I can be in this now moment

Tomorrow I will strive to be more then today and
then there will be rough days with whole's in
it

Such is life the flow, if nothing else I continue to grow

What a ride

Thoughts that smile

Think about all the things that make you
smile even if just for a little while

Let your heart feel light if only for a moment

The more we do it the more we grow it

Growth

You have inspired me to learn and grow was it easy No

Was it worth it Yes do I sit in regret No

In this on going process intended or not I'm
a better person then I was at the start

And just in case your wondering, Yes I feel the same

Up and down in and out through it all you
have always been more then a thought

Think think Think

Us over thinkers can over do it relax feel in to it

Feel a smile without over thinking trust it, not all smiles are a shiesty grin you'll know the difference you'll feel it within

Especially if it keeps coming around every now and then

Feeling's of Love

Love is patient love is kind not always easy at times

Love feels past all deceptions
misunderstandings it understands fear

Love is deep therefore repeats over in our hearts
through thick and thin waiting to start

Love can not be bought nor taught it just is

A true feeling that can't be fought or pushed away
it finds a place to rest and there it stays

Only Human

We all make mistakes need to give ourselves
a break, were only human

Corrections made brings peace to our days
do something you enjoy take a break

When we don't learn from our mistakes most likely they will
repeat some of us hard headed wondering why we can't sleep

Why is what I long for alluding me what is it I don't see

Think and feel into your life believe it will
be alright tomorrows a new day

In it all the light will come on you'll course correct
temper regret and don't be so hard on yourself

All will be fine make good use of life give it time

Anew

Detach from what burdens you in order to allow the new

We can't move forward when we stay in the
past no need to always look back

Rest play find joy in your day happy thoughts a grateful
heart trust that you'll receive what you want
You may not know the how when who or what keep the faith,
don't forget to do your part even if that's just to trust in yourself

The Minds Prison

We don't need to live in the prison of our mind

Break the chains that bind

Freedom of the mind only we can create we are
the jailer no need to escape just insert the key
to open the gate and set yourself free

Autumns Fantasy

A clear cool night looking at the stars reach
out and touch them they aren't that far

Laying under the stars on this cold Autumn night
seeing each others breath holding on tight

The rustling under blankets cozy and warm
our breath turns from cold to warm

Excited giddy from the rush of cold air
the passion grows hot explodes

Super Nova!

Gone Wrong

Do we think about how everything could
go wrong instead of right

Wouldn't it be better if we switched it around positive
thoughts brave actions surely creates positive attraction

They say like attracts like wouldn't it be
nice if we put down the struggle

Not saying we never have a negative thought but
if that's the reflex then all could get lost

Great outcomes come from I can do it
let not a negative past ruin it

Speak Up

What is it you need from me? Speak with clarity

To assume a person knows what one needs if
not spoken get's caught up in the weeds

We can all play our roles in harmony when
we express to each other what we need

Two capable people in this game of life can
have an ego battle if not set right

We most likely have different strengths
that can benefit a relationship

Inflamed Ego or Love

An out of balance ego creating fear I'll stay put I know what's
right here I believe I have control because this is what I know

Good or bad doesn't matter familiarity ego chatter

When no forward movement creates what
we thought our ego responds
"Aha I was right"

The sad truth is we question our feelings
stuck in our heads mind reeling

We manifested from our ego a missed
opportunity we wanted so much

I believe in this time and space a world out of
balance sometimes reflected on our face

Take off the mask follow your feelings your heart
will thank you, your soul is screaming

"Love conquers ALL" don't forget it's the main ingredient
to change the fall of self and therefore all else

Discouragement

Discouragement what is it's point to stop a
person walking towards what they want?

To altar a decision that one makes for themselves
what is the intention a question best felt

Of course there are times when it's needed more like
a teaching, the safety of a child so no harm comes
their way "don't play in traffic", surely a bad day

As adults to discern for ourselves should be respected
it's not for anyone else to try and direct

When another feels they know what's best for you ask
them to switch roles and stand in your shoes chances are
they won't want to be discouraged anymore then you

Awareness of intention should always come into
play but not if it's only to do it their way

Our decisions are ours and should be honored it's
our path to walk even if we encounter Piranhas
for how will we learn any other way it won't be
because someone told us don't do it, stay away

We gain wisdom from the good as well as the bad
not because some one told us stand back

Feel Into Thought

To much thinking we all do it believing it's how we get clear

Yet forgetting to feel into it then expecting it to magically
appear it doesn't show up then thinking why isn't it here

While stuck in our heads sitting in our chair it
can't come in no movement there we've all figured
out it doesn't magically appear, unless you're a
really good Magician and they are pretty rare

When we follow our feelings it can propel action
while only in thought a stagnant reaction

It always seems easier to stay put but is
it fulfilling as we tap our foot

Agendas Disinformation

Agendas disinformation what is the point

Is it to sway to convince to get your vote?

Do we listen to information without discernment
to blindly follow because we like the label

To follow a party line because that's what we've
supported or been around in our adult lifetime
does that make it true or so at this point in time

In this ever changing world this is the question I propose

Do we shut down our feelings and disseminate
information with only logic or the way it use to
be could this be a recipe for political unrest to the point of toxic

Remember the saying "that doesn't feel right"
when did we lose sight of that individual right

Group mentality has it's place think tanks problem solving
specifics put in place but not to control the entire human race

To force group mentality onto the entire human
race has created a world of division and strife
the only thing left is the need to be right

Must we be in opposition and to what end can we
ever get back to respecting our differences again

"The only constant is change" How can we
learn from one another when we stand in
opposition we need unity it's time let's start

One

Everything I write that comes in can apply
to so many a loved one a friend

Our experiences can be so similar yet varied in
ways we are all human each and every day

If you believe we are one then how can we not
understand what may come may choose to leave
again the circle of life does it repeat never end

In our now moments we can also feel the same
with variations as individuals the divine game

Our individual selves connected as one in this
game of life can be trying and fun

We the People

The many what have we survived have we done
our due diligence while accepting lies.
Have we had compassion for our fellow man ourselves kept
a happy loving attitude with the cards we've been dealt.
Did we work our entire lives just to be left did we defend
our country and then be left to care for ourselves.
Some broken and battered to fight for every
penny then get denied in a system of plenty.
I am a woman who has raised her children who
has worked who has cared for her spouse who
has supported herself in these later years
Governments Corporations that treat us with disregard
is not what we've paid into as life gets hard.
Our bodies no longer as resilient and strong are we
left to fight for what we've earned all along
This imbalance the greed of corporations making
more then what they need increasing their profit
margins when they've already succeeded.
Corporate greed look around what do you see is every
man and woman who has worked for you truly free.
Let us not forget "The American Dream" land of the free

Endings and Beginnings

Death the end comes in many forms either way leaves us forlorn

The end of a day as a new one begins
the loss of a loved one a friend

We can long for yesterdays as we greet a new tomorrow we
can long for a loved one gone yet keep moving forward

All is never forgotten yet can be missed mourned as
we heal our hearts for tomorrow will surely come

Emotional Space

I've not walked away I'm giving you space

I realize we operate in different ways

In that judgement I don't place just wishing
you'd feel comfortable to communicate

What you feel what you want I'm confused sometimes lost

Just because I say it all doesn't make you wrong

You may be confused in my absences doesn't
mean I don't feel the same as what I've expressed
just means at times I need to rest

I am emotional but clear in what I want then I carry
on taking care of life's demands and son on

Nothing here is wrong just holding space
wondering do we want the same outcome

Emotional Hostage

Let's not use another's emotions or words against them

We all have made decisions changed our mind
trying to figure out life over time

If expression is not received kindly then the hurt persists

No solution or understanding just remaining
defensive viewing it blindly

How do we know what another wants to say
if the chance isn't given day after day

Shutting down communication get's you nowhere
wouldn't it be nice to clear the air

In that place listen with compassion we've
all been there in our own actions

I am perfectly imperfect I've agreed to come
here to grow no regrets do I want in tow

If You Only Knew

If you only knew all I've written to you

I've wanted to respect your space doing
my best to stand in grace

I will not impose I will wait for that beautiful
love that's reflected on your face

I'll wait until I no longer can, won't wait
forever that's never the plan

It can be hard let there be no doubt takes two to figure this out

Partners in the Mud

Sometimes life gets tough I want a partner who's
not afraid to trudge through the mud

How sweet it will feel when we've gone down into
the depth where we struggled to catch our breath
and wondered will it ever get better then this

Not so serious waiting for the shoe to drop relax don't take the
shoe off, don't be so serious laugh a little you'd be surprised
how the crap can turn into a giggle then you start roaring
as if you've gone insane but it's truly funny is life a game

A partner in the dark as well as the light and in it
all we won't lose sight that with work put in
it will get bright again

Disappointment

Living in disappointment leaves us nowhere
can't go back can't move forward

Living in ones head self torture

Action of any kind at this point better then sitting in your mind

Change can not happen merely by thought
unless you can bend spoons and forks

Armor

I can feel through your tough exterior your
heart is so warm your passion on fire

You've been burned you armor up defending
yourself protecting your heart

No one permitted to enter no damage will I allow the pain I
endured will never be repeated even if I'm alone love depleted

Love isn't planned in it's own energy it stands the
more you resist it the stronger it gets an eventual
explosion taking down everything in it's path

Intense interactions intense emotions
eventually lead to an intense explosion

Easy isn't always the way sometimes the
struggles lead to the best days

The Return

I returned to the place where I came from
many changes under the moon and sun

I asked the Universe, God to set me free
not realizing how lonely it could be

I held myself in my arms no attachment no commitment
to any one free as a bird sang my own song

A Gypsy to wander and roam never in a
place long enough to call home

From each place I'd been I had grown something new to learn
to share looking back at each step I was suppose to be there

I do not live my life in regret I'd do it all over again and if I
did not walk this path I would of never come back to myself
home

Deceiving ones self

Do we perpetuate lies in our mind to feel justified

The biggest untruths may come from yourself
our ego not always our best friend

We can get in a state from past hurts that allow our mind
to continually blurt untruths in the form of assumptions

Needing all the answers when we may never have
all the answers and maybe they aren't ours to
have, does anyone truly have to answer to anyone
not unless it's agreed upon otherwise it's
an inquisition

It feels good to surrender and allow instead of
control not necessarily an easy road but well worth
it I'm sure, still working on that aren't we all

Let go of how the past dampens your happiness be present

No Victim Here

I'm not a victim whatever I've experienced I've allowed

I will no longer allow myself to feel as if I've been taken down

I am more empowered from this day forth
knowing what I know I stand proud

I remain a loving soul I will not be taken down

Watch out world here I come bigger and
brighter fueled by infinite love

Warrior of Love

I'm not passive anything but

I am a warrior but one of Love

I am emotional I feel for all, just in
decisions I make my own call

I tap into my heart the first step I do not stand in blind
judgement of another I contemplate and wonder

How do they feel what have they gone through and have
they healed if not I hope they do what is their life like with
compassion present these are the questions I feel are needed

Compassion my compass perspective a must
what have I learned from justice

"Judge not lest ye be judged"

Feeling into Words

Just say it so they say but the power of a word
could stop a conversation ruin someone's day yet
when you speak from love it's all you can do it's
not in what you said but your intention and
truth

What do you want to say that you haven't said
is it stressing you out in your head

Do you not believe that love understands the past
does not need to ruin your hearts plans

Unconditional love is forgiving and kind does not hold
you in regret it taught you what you do and don't want

The hardest lessons in life are the ones we grow from
the most they taught us what we do and don't want

We tend to struggle with wrong or right yet
viewed from a place of learning it can ignite
the hearts compassionate understanding

Peace how does that feel

Can we allow peace to wash over us when feeling emotional

It seems at times surrender comes after exhaustion

Taking a deep breath a moment to reflect don't
allow continuous swirling in your head

Imagining the worst over and again will only leave you drained

Sometimes in the unknown the mind justifies
just make sure it's not perpetuating lies

Relax breath bring yourself clarity tap into
your heart trust what you feel

Feminine & Masculine

I am not a feminist I am feminine what do I mean

I stand in soft nurturing strength I am assured I am
supportive at times step forward but mainly hold space I try
my best to stand in grace I'm never at the back of the line
nor do I stand behind I stand beside am loving and kind

I will not be controlled but I will be loved and
work together no push pull or tug

I believe that the man for me may take the
lead and by that this is what I mean

He is strong and caring not emotional like me but
that's ok because I feel I see I believe in him

Don't want his life to feel burdened therefore I'm
nurturing he is comfortable in who he is and
wants to be a protector of me I feel safe in his love it's sweet

Together in our roles we will naturally
flow he is he and I am me

We give and receive in good measure yet we don't
keep score it only creates stormy weather

I don't believe gender dictates these roles it's more
of a feeling a self knowing and so it goes

I respect individuality I support that stand
when we can be ourselves ain't it grand

Emotional

All emotions are meant to be felt remember
not to take them out on anyone else

Positive emotions surely needed negative
ones can leave you depleted

As we travel through the light and dark give
yourself a break trust in your heart

Wishes

Don't give up on your wish because you can't see
it keep the faith and remember you can feel it

Trust in divine timing there is more at
play so stop pining day after day

One foot in front of the other day by day
the Universe lights the way

What's meant for you will not go away it's
deep in your heart where it can stay

Free Will always at play

Teachers

Surrounded by teachers in this school of life some lessons
easy some hard growth assured in the remembrance of it all

Keep what serves you let the rest go the point of it all is
to forever expand I do believe that was part of the plan

Bumped my Head

Love – bumped my head a time or two but rose
to the top again still believing in it's truth

Love fills me up with knowing it feels good and
true couldn't hold it in even if I wanted to

My love is not a weapon nor given on a battlefield
it's given from the depth of my soul it's real

My passion burns bright deep into the night you
will feel the heat then refreshed by morning's
light

A blessing at times at times feels like a curse
I'll never stop loving even if it hurts

Fogs Reflection

The fog rolls in a reflection of what's been
waiting for the sun to appear again

Why wait when we can call in the sun
get up get out have some fun

The stormy weather was needed now it's over
move forward relax into the peace of it

Loves Options

You were never the option you were always the
choice in my heart from the day we met

My mind may not of always been sure
but my heart had always known

Over time I felt you again and again every
day every night in my heart we spent

Believing in Loves Mystery

I believe in love
I believe in his eyes
I believe in his unspoken words
I believe in his smile
I believe in me

I believe that we find that one person in
our lifetime who can be a mystery
I believe in the mystery of Love

Belief Reborn

To focus on the past is to lose the future
keep your future dreams alive
Trust what you feel as you lay in the darkness

Laying in the coffin to be reborn don't
allow your mind to be torn

Believe in new starts because it's not possible without the end

You can't see in the dark your physical senses disoriented
yet your emotions thoughts still present trust what you feel

You know more then they'd have you believe

Money can't buy Love

In my humble opinion time is precious money needed can't
enjoy it if you feel depleted no energy no time what's the point
From past experience a relationship of over
30 years worked himself into an unwell place
lost relationships he could not repair
I remember when our life was simple a special
place in time a good man he was and still is
Our childhood our upbringing what we've been
told all varies in how our life stories unfold
Some grew up in struggle some did not some
felt like money was the only way
Successful outcomes it's not all lost if we remember
to have fun before what's important is gone
Money is not wrong money is not bad unless
it's at the cost of your happiness, sad
An old saying "you can't buy love" does anyone truly think
about the meaning or shrug wonder why they feel empty
I have money I have stuff so why am I unhappy feel loss
What's missing a connection loneliness deep within
someone who cares about me and I them
I remember mom's fond memories of when times were
simple when she and dad first began they danced
in the living room played cards with friends not
worrying about money not much was coming in
They had each other more love then money
so sweet and simple pure as honey
If we constantly strive for more at what point is it enough at
what cost do we remember throughout life "we can't buy Love"

Guilty Decisions

Never rush into decisions based on guilt
breathe take time love yourself

If we surround ourselves with people who always want
to blame how will that serve us at the end of the day

Miscommunication or none at all can allow
something nice to crumble and fall

Corse correction needed speak from your hearts truth
trust when communicating from this place the best
intentions for each other is received in this loving space

Discernment

Discernment what does it mean taking knowledge
information teachings and feeling within?
Blindly following without this filter can lead to disillusionment
Doctrine Dogma outside information swallowed
without thought or feeling a dangerous road one
may not want to walk or tow and then again maybe
they do at the end of the day it's up to you
How do you feel about information imparted
is it given from a source that you feel has the
highest intention for you and all that is
Is it open ended or fixed
We were all given wonderful tools feelings
the mind a big part of our school
What may feel right to someone but not to you
are the differences that add to the jewl, Self
No need to lose ones self each path different it's
ok for we receive and create in various ways

Can always choose again

Can we forgive ourselves and choose again I believe so

Why live in regret when your heart says go

Is it not worth the answers you seek instead of swimming
in the deep the darkness the minds repeat

We miss so many things our heart desires
when surrounded by darkness and lies

Are we the ones that allowed this it's all right when this we face

We can always make the change we can always choose again

If we believe love conquers all brick by brick tear down the wall

First step forgive one's self and from that place forgive all else

Don't Stop

The work doesn't stop inner outer doesn't matter

Keep on growing no matter our age always new
knowing aha moments keep on rowing

At times pulling the oars out of the water flowing
no need to fight the current balance the two

Can't get it wrong when we keep on going
surrender to change trust your knowing

Love shrouded in Darkness

My love for you has never left at times shrouded in darkness

Those moments reminding us to come back to
self for how else could we love anyone else

I believe to be whole we experience life's
ups and downs the winding road

If it were easy how would we know how would we grow
to see life's beauty if we didn't know the absence of it

How could we truly feel it the polarities in life surely needed

Beginners Mind

If we want change a beginners mind comes into play

Leveling up getting it together at times
can feel like stormy weather

Staying grounded trust what you feel
soften the mind trust it's real

Get out in nature breathe surround yourself with trees

Animals a good release listen to the sounds the birds they speak

Time for self hand over all else if only for
a moment ground yourself breathe

Dear God Please

When we have a melt down it's not always pretty

Clearing out the darkness burning it down
releasing energies within don't want to drown

In this place not intending hurt just lost
it for a moment and out I blurt

Falling to my knees in order to stand again Dear God please

I needed help in this place with God I
pleaded guide me back to grace

I'm here within I've always been your
not alone you've never been

Just call on me in your darkest hour I'll lift you up you've
scraped your knees I'll brush them off you never have to plead

Your strong your loving can't you see every
experience brings you closer to me

Shift into receiving

Am I open to receive or just keep giving keep
on going what next I'm thinking

I've been the one who get's things done
it's how it's been not two but one

I take charge of my life I get it done make things
happen why do I feel something is lacking

I do it all because I can besides don't have
a man it's just me how I stand

Not much time for fun getting stuff done because I must

It sure would be nice to take a breath
do I realize I can ask for help

I look forward to a loving relationship solo
never suited me got love to give

Support in life support in love reciprocation two not one

All is possible can even be fun

Self imposed restrictions

Self imposed restrictions do we create propagate our own trap?

I know been there done that

Instead of following our heart taking action
our mind goes to what is lacking

When inspired take those steps just do
it quit thinking of what if's

Missed joys missing someone can we not get back to having fun

Be in the moment

Come Home

Hear me my dear there will be no battle here

Rest gain your strength then us we can address

I'm sorry you felt you had to go it alone when you are
ready come home I'll be waiting no longer without you

My battle was my worthiness I laid that down and healed myself

Together in peace and love we heal it's not over
walk through the door this is what we've been
fighting for

Come home

No more Push Pull

No more push pull for me I just want to be happy

Whatever that may be Universe I am happy
to receive nothing left to preconceive

I surrender and trust that Love will find me fill my cup
my course is simply to be love release and trust

Love life love what I do love being creative love another

Thank You

Love Light

I won't turn off my Love Light I will shine bright

Brighter each day illuminated by love

I've always felt it even if it was shrouded in darkness

Light illuminates the darkness even in
times of sorrow and despair

The light seeps in even when fuzzy and unclear
when we open our eyes and focus it's right there

The light dims at times then like a Phoenix ablaze
it rises again powerful strong it soars out of the
fog out of the haze it's fire light once more

Power Couple

Power Couple what does that mean is there
any emotion or are they just mean

Is Love present or is it only about gain win
at all cost kicking ass taking names

Is that at all fulfilling is it power over others do they
feel superior doesn't sound like much fun to me

Does that not burn them out left feeling exhausted
from wanting to stay at the top my question
is at the top of what and at what cost

Is it a partnership a team flowing in life is that what
it means? I hope so because sounds scary to me

I want to be a Power Couple of Love that sounds more fun not
so intense needing to stay at the top nonsense, when you place
yourself above some one else your looking down on another

Let me tell you friends that's not how this world will mend

Dizzy

You make me feel dizzy you make me feel
calm around you my heart sings a song

Your soft gentle presence in it's self a song

You temper yourself your strength so as not to scare me away

That's not possible because here I want to stay

You see I feel who you are a warm
strong star waiting to explode

Sweet peas

When giving from the heart nothing is small when
gifted from this place it is the love that makes it big
could of made you laugh by giving you a twig

Your smile went straight to my heart if sweet peas is all it takes
for you to smile I know without a doubt you are my guy

Your kind your caring you created the vase as you
poured the water and put them in place the sweet
peas and you brought a smile to my face

Simple touching moments the biggest gifts couldn't ask
for anything more then the smile from your lips

Some day we'll have more time

The little things you do the way you move the attention
you give when I speak I can't stop thinking of you

Imagining someday we'll have more time
it's simple your always on my mind

I take a walk as I move I look for you everywhere
waiting for you to magically appear

I feel like your with me and maybe you
are I know I feel you in my heart

I'll continue to wish upon a star and then like
magic there you are there you'll be

Opposites

Have you ever resonated with someone
opposite of you and wondered why

Are you looking for truths or answers that
from your perspective alluded you

Polar opposites coming together may create a
balance in one another of course if your open to
receive not just firing off what you believe

In metaphysics alchemy zero point the
center is where you have epiphanies

For growth and expansion in relationship I believe
the opposite of you could be the trick if you allow

Possibly a divine Union created somehow?

Change the unknown

Why do we fear change probably because
we don't know what's up ahead

Instead I'll just lay in bed

No risk can make us mentally emotionally and physically sick

There are no guarantees in life except death and then
you choose to start over again be this a metaphor or
actual self it doesn't matter change none the less

Wouldn't it be nice to see if what your feeling can end
up being your dreams the best change it just might be

Peace and quiet

The lines the roadmaps on my face I haven't earned in grace

I'm always growing in my knowing that
I agreed to be where I am

It's always my choice to use my voice and
know when words aren't helpful

Silence is underrated a trait I've not
embraced but now I'm learning to
stand in grace

Printed in the United States
by Baker & Taylor Publisher Services